YOU CAN FLY, LITTLE BIRD

You Can Fly, Little Bird

Story by *Tuula Pere*
Illustrations by *Alexandra Burda*
Layout by *Peter Stone*
English translation by *Päivi Vuoriaro*
Edited in English by *Susan Korman*

Copyright © 2018 Wickwick Ltd
Helsinki, Finland

Published by Wickwick Ltd, 2018

Originally published in Finland by Wickwick Ltd in 2018
Finnish "Osaat lentää, lintu pieni", ISBN 978-952-325-411-4
English "You Can Fly, Little Bird", ISBN 978-952-325-412-1

You Can Fly, Little Bird

TUULA PERE · ALEXANDRA BURDA

WickWick
Children's Books from the Heart

On a slope near a forest grew a huge tree. Its branches gave shelter to many kinds of birds who had chosen it as their nesting tree.

On the sturdier branches near the trunk, larger birds made their nests, while the sparrows nested along the dense, thinner branches. A few bird families had even chiseled out burrows in the rotten treetop.

"Isn't it wonderful that we chose this particular tree?" a father bird said to his mate. "From here we have the best view in the entire forest."

The mother bird nodded contentedly, admiring the newly finished nest. Then she set herself in a comfortable position. It was time to start laying eggs.

S oon three brindled eggs lay in the nest. The parent birds took turns brooding them, making sure that they remained warm all the time. At night, when it grew chilly, they carefully covered each egg under the soft feathers of their bellies.

"I wonder what our chicks will be like." The birds pondered the thought together. "Will they be quiet or wild? Will they quickly learn how to fly?"

"Well, one thing's for sure. They will be brindled like us," Mother said.

"I suspect none of them is going to be much of a singer—if they take after me, that is," Father reckoned.

After days of brooding, it was time for the chicks to hatch.

A crack appeared on two eggs almost at the same time. Tiny beaks broke through the shells first, and then slowly but determinedly, two wet chick bodies broke free. This meant busy times for the parent birds. The hatched chicks were constantly hungry.

Meanwhile the shell of the third egg remained intact. Mother was getting worried about the delayed arrival of her lastborn.

After a few days of impatient waiting, the last chick hatched.

"I guess our lastborn is more cautious and slower than the others," Mother said, gently stroking the tiny chick with her wing. "Let's name her Serene."

"Serene seems to be quite timid," Father said. "Look how she gets startled even by her own siblings."

Little by little, the smallest chick got used to being in the noisy, crowded nest. Being much weaker and slower than her siblings, she sometimes had trouble getting her share of the food their parents brought to the nest. Fortunately, Mother and Father made sure that Serene had her tummy full of insects and worms too.

One day Serene cautiously peeked over the side of the nest. Between the tree branches, she saw more and more trees. The blue sky glimmered high above. Sounds came from every direction; the wind stirred the branches; and birds of different sizes flitted past the nest. Scents filled the air.

The little bird started to feel dizzy. How immense the world seemed!

How will I ever have the courage to leave the nest? Serene thought, frightened. *The other chicks have already started practicing flight movements.*

Serene listened anxiously to her siblings making plans for their first flight.

"I will fly straight down to the valley and soar as far as I can," the oldest chick declared.

"The wind is stronger higher up on the hill. I want to swirl in the air," the middle one added, full of excitement.

"I don't want to go anywhere yet," Serene said quietly. "Last night I heard some strange noises. And on top of the tree next to ours, I saw a frightening creature with big yellow eyes. I don't want to come face to face with it."

"Dear child, it was our neighbor, the night owl," Mother reassured her. "He stays up all night and hoots into the dark."

The next day, the first chick took off for her trip. The others watched, admiring how she spread her wings and headed down. After a little fluttering, she soon managed to catch the wind and soar with it—away from sight.

After a while, she returned—out of breath—and told the others about her exciting experiences.

"I saw a monster with long legs and a pointy beak. It almost walked over me when I was resting on a stone by the pond!"

"That's a wader," Mother explained. "A wader has long legs. It uses them to get through damp and muddy places. With its long beak, a wader catches fish from the water and frogs from the shore grass."

14

The oldest chick had seen more amazing things.

"I saw a bird plunge into the water. It stayed there so long, I started to worry it might drown!"

"That was a diver bird. They know how to dive under the water and catch fish," Father said. "But you mustn't try the same thing. Insects, grains, and berries will do fine for us little birds."

Luckily, I will not have to learn how to dive, Serene thought. *Even flying scares me.*

A new morning dawned, and the middle chick was ready to fly. He bounced off the ledge of the nest and flapped his wings furiously. Soon he was in the air, wobbling toward the top of the hill.

Serene stayed in the nest to practice. She flitted from side to side, but her wings could not quite get wind beneath them. Embarrassed, she found herself crawling up from the bottom of the nest time after time.

In the afternoon, the middle chick returned home.

"It was so great!" he said. "At first, I was frightened, but then I let myself go in the wind swirls."

Mother frowned gently. "Please keep in mind that you are not a hawk or a swallow. Those birds are born to shoot down a cliff. Our wings are not as strong and swift as theirs."

Serene decided that if she ever learned how to fly, she would stay in her home forest, under the shelter of the trees. That alone was exciting enough.

Serene kept practicing. Her parents patiently brought her food to the nest. Slowly, she began to rely on her wings. The youngest chick grew stronger and braver— now she even dared to stand up straight on the ledge of the nest!

"Today is my turn," Serene said decidedly. "I, too, want to see amazing things, although I'm sure I'll find them in our home forest as well."

Serene took one last anxious glance at her mother, and then raised herself on her wings.

Serene was happy. Despite being so tiny and timid, she knew how to fly now! The air felt thick and soft as it gently carried the young bird. After her initial hesitation, she was already quite a good flier. Serene was especially good at darting between the trees.

"How different the dwellers in our home forest are!" Serene marveled. "I never imagined there'd be so many sorts of birds."

On her flight, she encountered small and large birds, slow and fast fliers. Some of them could sing intricate melodies, while others croaked coarsely.

After returning to her home nest, Serene was beside herself with excitement when she told the others what she had seen. She was particularly amazed by the colorful birds and the songs she had heard.

"Mom, could you teach me how to sing more beautifully?" Serene asked. "I heard songs that were incredibly beautiful."

"My child, you have your own distinct voice, and it's just fine," her mother said. "And that voice is just perfect for joining the choir of other birds and singing along with them."

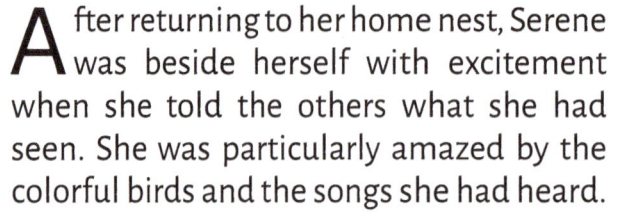
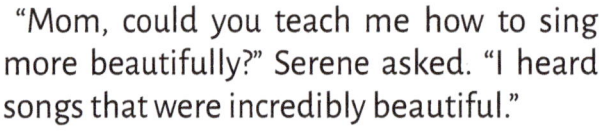

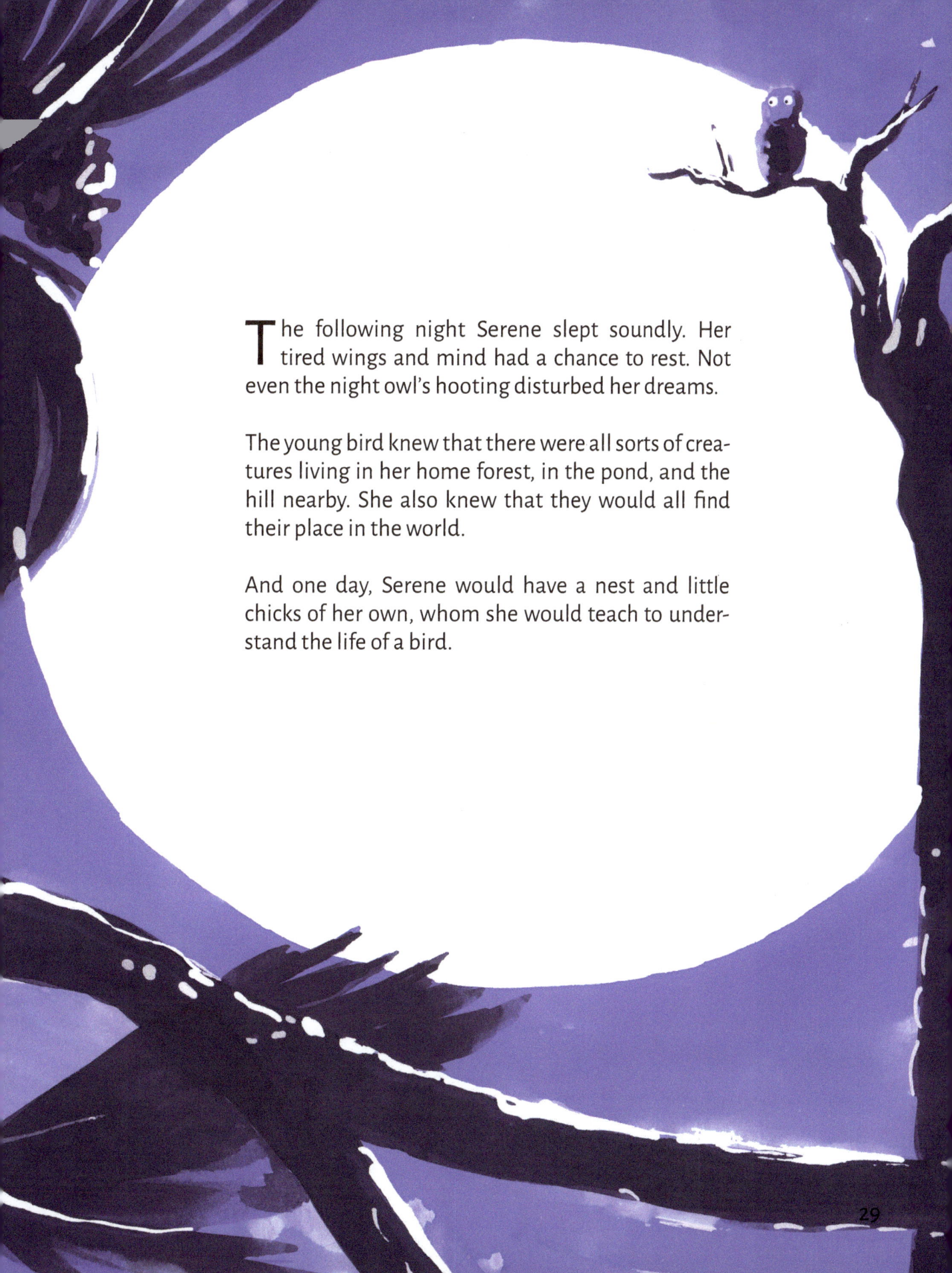

The following night Serene slept soundly. Her tired wings and mind had a chance to rest. Not even the night owl's hooting disturbed her dreams.

The young bird knew that there were all sorts of creatures living in her home forest, in the pond, and the hill nearby. She also knew that they would all find their place in the world.

And one day, Serene would have a nest and little chicks of her own, whom she would teach to understand the life of a bird.

www.ingramcontent.com/pod-product-compliance
Lightning Source LLC
Chambersburg PA
CBHW041156120626
46547CB00020B/3236